How to Gain Confidence as a Rider

Copyright © 2016 Sunny Hale

All rights reserved. No part of this work may be reproduced in any form without the written consent of its author.

www.sunnyhalepolo.com

DEDICATION

To all the great horses, who helped me conquer my dream in the sport of Polo and to discover the true meaning of life in the process, this is for you. I hope it helps other people truly understand the magnificent language a horse is speaking and the gift that is waiting in the journey to becoming a confident equestrian. You are amazing and priceless gifts to this world and I appreciate every one of you who has given me so much. I want to say a special thank you to the horses that worked the hardest to get my attention and explain your message, you know who you are. Thank you for your persistence and your patience, I will forever be grateful for all you taught me and all we experienced on the journey. It is the gift of a lifetime.

In gratitude always,

Sunny

For more books by Sunny Hale
or to learn more about her go to:

www.sunnyhalepolo.com

How to Gain Confidence

as a Rider

A Champion's guide to understanding and overcoming your fears

Sunny Hale

CONTENTS

1. Listen close…   1-2

2. A personal note from the horse   3-4

3. What it's going to take   5-8

4. Confidence is a process   9-26

5. The Truth   27-36

6. Trust the process   37-44

7. New habits that will help you   45-54

8. Enjoy the ride   55-60

9. About the author   61-66

How to Gain Confidence as a Rider

CHAPTER ONE

Listen close…

My goal with this book is to help you understand and overcome your confidence issues with horses by explaining the things I learned along the way in my professional career. These facts helped me conquer my dream in the sport of Polo, which is over 2,000 years old and had never seen anything like what I wanted to do. It took serious confidence on the back of horse to do it and the lessons I learned in the process were priceless and what I am going to share with you here. This information is directly as I learned it and like no other book you will read on the subject. Get ready, as some of it might be a shock to you to learn, but what it will do is provide you with a whole new angle you never thought of or realized about the character of a horse that affects your confidence. I guarantee you this one fact. After you read this book you will no longer be able to say, "I have no idea how to solve the issue that is happening to me", anymore. You will now have some solid information and personal tools that you can start using to erase previous confidence issues.

Now get busy, good luck!

Sunny

CHAPTER TWO

A PERSONAL NOTE FROM THE HORSE

I am an amazing animal with unlimited powers to enhance your day each time you come to see me. I am magic on hoofs. However, I require one thing. Please take the time to understand and gain as much knowledge as you can about what makes me happy and what upsets me. If you will just give us time to get to know each other and build some trust, I am truly wanting to be loyal and do all I can in pursuit of your personal goals on my back, no matter what discipline or hobby you would like me to participate in. I can do hundreds of things like jump, race, trail ride, swim, cut cows, run reining patterns, carry camping gear to the mountains, check fence lines, doctor cattle, play polo, do dressage, eat all your money, pull carriages, provide therapy for people, be your best friend, barrel race, play polocrosse, carry policeman through the city, be your confidant after a hard day at the office…you name it I can do it. If you will just give me time to understand what you are asking of me and time to learn to trust you, I will be your most loyal and powerful friend in our journey to accomplish your goal.

I also want you to know, that if you get in a hurry and try to force your will on me without clearly explaining what you want or before you have earned my trust, there is a good chance you will eat some dirt. Sorry, but I can't help it that's just the way I'm made. I will do my best to understand the language you are speaking to me by your actions and I hope you will take some time to understand the language I speak, by my actions.

Please read this book carefully and when you're done, I look forward to having a great ride. Remember, I am magic to the soul when we can communicate properly. You will feel invincible and so will I, as we go after our goal together. I look forward to hearing from you soon ☺!

CHAPTER THREE

WHAT IT'S GOING TO TAKE

Gaining confidence as a rider starts with one decision. You have to be ready to make a commitment that you are going to solve your fears or doubts. That is the catalyst that will put everything else in motion. Without that one decision to commit as your foundation, you will constantly be plagued with doubt owning the number one real estate plot in your mind and it will continue to resurface at the worst of times.

I tell you this advice right in the beginning for a reason. My aim in this book is to give you solid advice that I know works, when it comes to riding horses. These are lessons learned from my own experiences and from helping others around the world with overcoming their doubts and fears on the back of a horse. Solid advice that can truly help you is often the hardest to hear or comprehend. The reason it is so hard to hear or comprehend, is that you already have years and years of the same message or thoughts running through your mind about your experiences that you are used to and it takes time and physical practice to identify, unravel and replace them.

If you truly want to pull the plug on your doubts and fears when you ride, you have to realize it starts in your mind. You need to make that commitment to own the real estate in your mind with this new statement. "I am going to solve these doubts, they are no longer going to own me." That will be your new personal internal message to replace the old one that said, "your doomed." It's that simple. That's where it starts. This and the practice of new habits and some new things I will show you in this book, is what it will take to gain the confidence you are looking for. The kind of confidence we are going for is the kind that will be lasting and powerful in your riding experience.

Are you ready to make the commitment? If your immediate answer to yourself when you read that question…and yes IMMEDIATE ANSWER to that question was, "I don't know about that" "she doesn't know what happened to me" "yeah, but I've had this fear from a bad accident" you need to realize, that is how much of a hold those doubts have on your thought process. Take notice of what was your immediate answer and who owns the number one real estate plot in your mind right now…doubt. That internal message may be stuck on "auto reply". That is the source of the message we are after in this book. That is the one we are going to uproot. Trust me I know what you're thinking, because I have been there. I overcame those kinds of messages and so can you.

Gaining confidence as a rider starts with that one decision. You have to be ready to make a commitment that you are going to solve your fears or doubts. Making this one decision and new commitment to yourself as your new foundation, will change everything for you. This commitment means you are ready to start doing the work to erase those doubts and fears and start replacing them with new habits and messaging that I am going to show you in this book.

This new commitment and personal message, "I am going to solve these doubts, they are no longer going to own me", will also become your Rule #1 and foundation to return to, if at any point things flare up down the road and threaten to challenge your progress. Now you will have something to fight back with. This will help you set everything back in motion and you right back on the path to success. This is your own personal gift you can give yourself…for free ☺!

The longer you wait to make this first and most important decision, the longer fear and doubts get to own you and the real estate in your mind. I suggest you pull the trigger on this decision now, but it is up to you to decide.

Sunny Hale

CHAPTER FOUR

CONFIDENCE IS A PROCESS

As a rider, there are a few key things you need to know when it comes to having and building confidence. For me it boils down to a process of four main steps that you will want to learn to master over time. You may already have mastered one or more of them in your current riding ability, but if you are missing any one of these steps, that may be where you are running into issues and your confidence is draining out. My goal in this book is to give you new tools to apply to your situation so you can fix the leaks!

This process I am going to explain takes time and it takes a willingness to realize, you hold the answers to your own success. How much you gain is completely in your own hands once you have the knowledge I am going to give you.

Sunny Hale

STEP ONE

Gaining confidence starts with one decision.

You have to be ready to make a commitment that you are going to solve your fears or doubts. This one decision is the catalyst that will put everything else in motion. Make this decision " I am going to solve my doubts and fears, this is it…I AM going to do it", your new personal anthem. Repeat it to yourself often. Spend a few minutes each ride with that thought in your mind. Let it sit there, let it own some space in your mind and thoughts and watch it grow. It is up to you to plant the seed. Plant it and then water it by giving it time to exist in your mind. Keep it handy when you go to the barn and when you start to feel any reminder of the old messaging pop into your mind. This is step one and needs to be repeated until it becomes your new internal message. Especially if you are just starting out in the process to solving your confidence issue, pay attention to this one decision and message. It will begin to drive everything forward in the right direction. Once you decide to make this commitment and take this step, you will be firmly headed in the right direction to becoming a more confident rider.

In this part of the process, expect that you are going to have days that challenge you. Each new experience or old one that pops up that questions you is nothing more than a test to see how you are doing in your new commitment. Don't fall for the old message anymore. That was before you were armed with this info and plan. Get ready to whip out your new anthem at the first sign of trouble and keep repeating it until it is your first response to all scary situations and becomes your new habit. Expect to be challenged and remember, this is a necessary step you will need to take and keep retaking until all of the old messaging that was causing you trouble is gone...for good.

STEP TWO

*A horse speaks a language…
you need to learn it.*

This is the next greatest element and step you need to know when it comes to gaining confidence as a rider. This is a fact you may not be aware of or never realized played such an important role in your confidence. Understanding that horses truly have a way of communicating and it is through their actions, all of them, will help you become a much more confident rider over time. A huge portion of self confidence in a rider, comes from knowing how to interpret the message the horse is sending you by their movements and actions, both on their back and on the ground leading up to the ride. Not knowing this language is the root of where most doubts live, because you are not sure or may be completely unaware of what is coming next in their movements.

Everything a horse does is an indication of their mood, their comfort level, their fears, their soundness or lack of, their trust, their fears, their doubts, their previous experiences, their awareness of their surroundings, their confidence, the potential dangers they are sensing, their level of like or dislike for you…all of it is rolled up into a language they speak. Everything a horse does is for a reason. Stuff doesn't just happen without any cause or reason and they always announce what's about to happen by their actions. Sometimes the actions are loud with abrupt and obvious movements and sometimes they are barely noticeable, but they all mean something. Something is about to happen next. This is the language you need to start studying each time you interact with a horse. They will teach you the language if you are willing to listen and let the conversation have two sides.

Once you start to pick up on this language you will have a much better chance of reading the situations you are in with a horse and being able to predict what is next. That is one of the largest keys to confidence as a rider.

The better you can become at reading their language, both body and mind, the better off you will be as a rider. Knowing what to expect by learning their character and the language they speak will make all of the difference in the world, in terms of confidence for you. Not knowing the language is when you will feel like a passenger on a double decker tour bus ride with someone else driving versus knowing the language, which is like driving a finely tuned Porsche through a racecourse you signed up for. Your knowledge will make this large of a difference in your capability to have an effect on the situation you are in. Just because you learned how to ride the top of the horse and hang on, does not mean you are a confident rider. Becoming a confidant rider takes learning the language of the horse and its character, so that you can be an active positive influence in the scene as it unfolds, no matter where you go riding. Do not be scared of the language by their actions just learn to speak it, even if it's only one word and action at a time that you can take on. This is one of the most rewarding steps in the process, as you start to pick up on what a horse is trying to say to you.

Sunny Hale

STEP THREE

Identify the source and cause of your fears

Do you know why it happened in the first place? What actually started the nervousness or build up of fears that took your confidence? Answering those two questions is where you need to start to solve the fears. It is extremely important to identify what is causing the lack of confidence. You may already know clearly, but there may be a few of you who haven't really stopped to think of why or where it all started. It is important to determine where exactly it all started and how long this has been allowed to live within you. Once you have those answers you can break the size of what you are dealing with, down into manageable parts that can be addressed over time. But without that knowledge, you will always be fighting this giant dark spot that seems huge and unstoppable. It is stoppable and it is curable with the right knowledge and work.

When you have genuine fear, you have to take a serious look at the cause and then take a step back to start to address the issues that the fear has created, one small step at a time. If you are in that scenario, do not be in a hurry to solve it. That is where taking your time to understand the situation fully and gather information, is key to solving the issue. Take your time on this step and write them down as you discover them if necessary. Once you can actually state to yourself what is the cause, you are then ready to start erasing the effects of the "old incident". Without that knowledge planted clearly in your mind, you will be like a gardener wearing a blindfold who is trying to water thirsty flowers in a huge garden. Plenty of good water is flowing, but you will have no idea of what you are aiming at. That is most likely why previous good efforts on your part, haven't produced the lasting results you are looking for. You have to know what you are aiming at, when you want to remove something.

STEP FOUR

Know what to do and how to handle the situations you will get in with a horse.

One of the most important things I have learned in my career with horses is that confidence comes with knowledge (knowing what to do) and practice of that knowledge (how to handle the situation). The combination of those two things leads to equestrian wisdom. There is no way around it…those are the facts. The more knowledge you can gain, the more confident you will become. The more you practice the knowledge you gain, the stronger your skills and bravery will become. This part of the process takes time to master and is actually your journey with horses and will continue throughout your life each time you work with a horse.

When I say knowledge, I also mean a wide variety of things that all pertain to the horse, both on the ground and on their back. The more knowledge you have, the less your mind is filled with doubt. Doubt in your mind comes from unanswered questions that you have in your private thoughts. These unanswered questions cause you to worry about the outcome of what you are doing.

When you ride or work around horses, a horse is going to ask you a question in their actions and it is up to you to know the answer to the question (knowledge) and then it is up to you to be able to execute the correct action to proceed (how to handle the situation). These are the elements and step that takes time and experiences to grow. This step happens each and every time you go to the barn or get on the back of a horse. Having these two elements does not happen instantly and don't let anyone fool you into believing it does. A good trainer will show you techniques to keep a horse's mind occupied, but at some point the horse will catch on unless you can show them consistently in your actions, that you mean what you are asking and can be trusted. This is a big step to reach and be able to take on your own, but it is one of the most rewarding steps in the process of becoming a confident rider.

I also want you to understand clearly, that when I say an "answer to a question" that presents itself with a horse, I am also talking about the physical reaction and skills that need to happen in answering the question that was presented. Most all of the times I fell off in my career as a youngster training horses, was because I was unprepared for what unfolded in my reaction (didn't have the answer how to handle the situation). I did not have enough skills and experience yet, to have predicted what was coming if I put a horse into a position or situation they weren't ready for. Your question to the horse in your actions has to match your skill level to respond, because if it doesn't you will be in for a ride that you don't know what to do about. It took me years before I knew how to deal with young horses who for no reason, so it seemed at the time in my experience level, from a nice calm sleepy walk would bolt like their tail was on fire and flipping out like I was the match that started it. Yes trust me I have had some hell rides, but each one taught me something I didn't know and especially in the areas of how to handle situations with random mysteries. This takes time and experiences on the back of a horse to learn.

Knowledge comes with practice. Rome wasn't built in a day and neither will your horse knowledge happen in a day. Knowledge about horses comes from spending time around them and physically experiencing the rush of it all. The more time you can spend in the saddle and around horses the more knowledge you will gain. Over time this knowledge adds up to the vaccine for your fear.

Think of this analogy. An MMA fighter or boxer has to know the right answer (knowledge) when a fighter throws a punch or kick at them. Part of knowing the right answer to defend themselves is knowing physically what to do about it (how to handle the situation). They spend a lot of time and sweat learning each and every correct answer necessary for everything that could potentially be thrown at them in a fight. Until one day, after years and hours of hard work on understanding and practicing physically to execute the specific details, they have all the answers and are a great fighter. They are a great fighter, because they know how to respond mentally and physically to all the situations that might come up in a fight. What they learned to solve in all of those hours at the gym shadow boxing and training, was mental and physical answers to all the unknowns that needed a solid answer. That is the best analogy I can think of when it comes to understanding that a horse is asking you a question in each and every one of the moves they make. They are opening a conversation with you by each move. Your knowledge of the right answers to the question, both mentally and physically in your actions and reactions, is where your confidence comes in to play. They are able to read your response to the question they presented you, by your energy, your physical movements or lack of response. If you have a lack of confidence, because you are unsure of what to do when the question is asked by the horse, you will hesitate and then the horse has the answer they needed and proceeds accordingly. "The person doesn't know or is not sure and I am on my own in how I respond with no guidance, but my own self-preservation or happiness", is what the horse just said. Then the adventure begins, with you in the backseat no longer driving, only you don't know it.

That is why it is so important to start working on each of these steps and especially this one, because it is the answer to strengthen your riding and confidence.

One of the most common issues that cause a lack of confidence is from not knowing what the answers are for a situation that presents itself with a horse, either mentally or physically. This can happen to everyone and does at one time or another along the way. Each time a situation comes up that you don't have the right answer for, you will be filled with fear and doubt. This fear and doubt is a blank space within you that is screaming for answers and the body's natural reaction is to avoid it or physically lock up, because you don't know what to do about it. This can be solved through time and efforts spent at learning what the answers are for the situation you are trying to have with the horse. Maybe it is learning to ride properly. Maybe it is learning to hang on better when things get faster. Maybe it is learning to be able to focus where you are going instead of at the horse's neck or mane for hints of movements. Maybe it is learning to focus on your destination instead of the ground. Maybe it is learning to slow down in your movements around a new horse. Maybe it is learning how to ride a horse that gets frisky in the cold weather. Maybe it is learning to handle a horse properly on the ground. Maybe it is just to be able to know how to be around them safely. Whatever it is, it is very much up to you how long this lack of answers and doubt gets to remain. Once you set your mind to solving the unknown, you will be on your way to a new found confidence.

Starting small is your biggest best move in this step of the process. Make sure to take small steps that are achievable and that bring you confidence, before jumping in too much deeper. Going too fast and especially in an area you are already having doubts about, will only escalate the size of a fear. Start small and add lost of positive small steps and you will be amazed at what begins to happen for you.

Always remember, you have to have those two elements to have equestrian wisdom. Without those two elements you will always have a space of unknown that still haunts you. So go to work on gaining as much knowledge as you can and then as many experiences as you can to apply the knowledge. Be prepared to keep practicing this step and remind yourself this is a process. You have to first collect the knowledge and then you have to put it to use in your experiences on the back of a horse, in order for it to sink in. Good luck and get to work, this step is the fun part for sure. You are enrolled at the school of horse and trust me when I say there is a lot to learn, but that is what being a confident rider is all about. It is a process and this is a huge step in that process. This is what horse trainers give their lives to for the passion it provides, so enjoy your journey it will bring you gifts you never imagined. That is part of the magic a horse possesses.

Sunny Hale

CHAPTER FIVE

THE TRUTH

Everything has a warning label, so here is the biggest one you should be aware of when you are working with horses. Do not forget this and realize I am stating these facts right in the beginning not to freak you out, but to help you understand clearly that not all horses are meant for everyone. If you have already experienced what I am about to explain and is the reason for picking up this book, then you will be especially happy to realize that whatever happened that caused you to lose some confidence may be very solvable and may have actually been the result of a simple mistake that is very easy to fix. If you are new to working with horses, then please pay very close attention to this chapter as it may help you avoid a very common mistake that happens to a lot of people.

If you are having major confidence issues than it may be a result of trying repeatedly to master riding only the top of the horse. Knowing the character of a horse, what makes them tick and how they express themselves is the key to your security and confidence on their back. Knowing each of those things will help identify what kind of horse you are working with.

Here is a fact to know. You are not meant for every horse and every horse is not meant for you. Stop fooling yourself or letting anyone else convince you of thinking you are an exact fit for every horse you will come across. A great rider even has limitations as to what type of horse they are best suited to work with. Example: a top-level equestrian jump or dressage rider no matter how high level they are…even at the Olympic level…is not going to ride or choose to ride a shaggy and wild bareback bronc from the NFR. Now, a cowboy on his way up the ranks in the NFR will be happy to draw the rankest one in the bunch and he's got a shot to actually ride it in style. That is an extreme example, but I want to make my point crystal clear to you, so that you can begin to understand that certain horses are suited for certain types of riders and their skill level. This is a mistake that can be avoided with some proper education about your skill level and the type of horse you are attempting to ride or work with. The mismatch of the two causes trouble every time. I am going to repeat this one single message throughout the book so that you start to pay attention to it in all your rides. You are not John Wayne and every horse is not Mr. Ed.

Beware of monsters in horse suits…

Yep, they do exit. Somebody has to tell you the truth and it may be what helps you avoid a bad situation so listen closely. There are a few bad apples in the bunch, just like people there are a few out there hidden in the crowd, so watch out for them. There are some horses out there that just would prefer to remain wild and untouchable. They like it that way and will do everything in their power to not have to change their way of life and thinking. This type of horse will speak LOUDLY through their actions and repeated attempts to destroy your plans with sneaky dangerous moves that appear to be attempts on your life. Don't make a mistake, they are, that horse means it. That horse is trying to get his or her point across to you. The harder you push your will on that type of horse, the louder their reactions will get. Wake up, not all horses are meant to be ridden. Some are meant to be wild. Learn to watch for the signs of a horse that falls in this category, it could save your life. The majority of horses are not this way, but don't think that every horse is like the movies and wants you to ride them and will hang around in the middle of the desert when you drop the reins and get off. Some won't ever allow anything on their backs, but the hair that is growing there now. Those kinds of horses do not want your help and are just fine to be who they are without you riding them.

Beware, monsters in horse suits kick…hard…and they mean it. They don't want to be touched. In fact, they will do anything and everything they can to get you to leave them alone. Beware…they aim to end the touching and friendship unless you are a highly skilled horseman who knows how to speak to them quietly and patiently. So if you don't have that kind of experience, please find someone who does, who can comprehend what that horse needs. You both will be better off until you have a clear understanding of the level of horsemanship this type of horse requires.

Horses who require professional help…

Some horses are very similar to people in that they have been betrayed or terrorized in previous relationships and or events in their life. Someone then tags them as a monster or crazy horse to watch out for. Those types of horses are generally freaked out when you present certain scenarios to them that they had a horrible previous experience with. You may or may not be aware of this internal fear that is buried deep within them. They will speak to you how they feel about it by their actions to act like a monster instead of a horse, in certain scenarios. What they are actually saying by their behaviors is that they need to get out of this situation that reminds them of the past and what hurt or freaked them out before. This is their natural way of protecting themselves and it needs to happen right away if they want to save themselves from more trauma. That is why the physical reaction they have is immediate, powerful, hard and fast. They might attempt to bolt like a runaway train, to dart the other way, to buck you off, to run you over or they might just refuse to leave the barn completely. Recognize that this type of horse needs a skilled professional who can help translate what their fears are and then create workable solutions to help them regain confidence and a reason to trust a person again. This type of horse will need to be taught to reface their fears slowly and relearn how to trust, before they are suitable for anyone to ask anything of them again and especially not from an inexperienced rider.

It is important to recognize if you have a horse that matches this description, because it causes major confidence issue in tons of riders. Especially when the horse has been sold to a rider who has no clue of the previous history the horse comes with. This type of mismatch can lead to a worse situation if left untreated. Matching a horse like I am explaining with an un-experienced rider or handler is a dangerous mix and literally like waiting for a plane to crash in the power of what can go wrong. I explain this to you, because it is one of the absolute easiest things to fix and all too common of a story among horse people.

Everyone has a story of a crazy situation they have been in, that usually amounts to a serious mismatch in the skill level required in a horse needs versus the human's knowledge of the correct answer and ability to execute when the question was presented by the horse. Let me make this point really clear. What would happen if you put a 2-year-old baby human, that is all about new things and being touchy feely with what fascinates them, in a cage with a lion? Exactly. Now, what would happen if you put a skilled lion trainer in the same cage with that lion? That is my point. At least the skilled lion trainer would have a chance to know the right reaction when the lion takes the first look at them. Harsh I know, but someone has to help you realize the power of a horse and just what you are doing to yourself if you assume you are the only one in the conversation. In every move a horse makes, they are speaking to you. You need to know the answer to the question and make a decision or the horse will make one for you. What they rely on is your response, so they can make their next move. In a horse that has been freaked out previously, they need to know the answer fast and they need to know they can trust what you are saying, because the last person didn't provide that. That is why there are some horses who require a professional who can assess what the horse is saying in the intensity or severity of their re actions to certain events they are introduced to. A good trainer will be able to interpret what the horse is saying or how severe the issue was or still is in the horse's mind. This is the dance I will explain later, but for now just know that horses are powerful and you need to always be respectful of what they can do as a first priority. If the situation you are in is not getting better and you can not get to a place of confidence with your horse in certain situations, you may need to get the horse professional help so you can get to the correct solution for both of you.

Sunny Hale

Be wise enough to know the difference...

Please start to pay attention to the fact that there is a big difference between a troubled horse, who just needs a chance to recover in the safety of a skilled horseman who knows how to speak the language of "I'm scared please help me", and a horse who is a monster and wants to harm you because you are threatening their freedom. There is a big difference and you need to always keep that in mind. It takes time to be able to know how to read the difference. That single piece of knowledge may be the barrier to previously unsolvable confidence issues with a particular horse or horse type that you have been riding or the actual cause of your original issue.

What I have just explained is a key piece of information in the process that you need to be aware of, as you may be attempting to tackle a monster that needs a more skilled equestrian. The more time you spend in the mismatch unaware of the situation, the greater the potential to kill your confidence all together if it goes too long with you getting hurt or scared with no sign of hope in sight that things will improve. That's why it's so important to understand the entire equation that makes up the word fear and to understand it comes from many sources. Once you are able to start identifying the sources you can start to conquer the issue one small step at a time. Start thinking through your scenario and see if maybe the issue is a mismatch for your current skill level? This can be a great motivator and slice of hope just to recognize this one small detail that is very fixable.

Pay attention to what I have explained in this chapter closely, because these are facts not too many people will tell you or take the time to explain properly. This information usually comes into a rider's awareness too late or never at all and the dangers they put themselves in as a result are far too costly when they don't even need to happen in the first place. If you will take some time to prepare yourself with solid information when you start, about the type of horse you are dealing with, it will help you avoid some serious mistakes and setbacks. That is my point for giving you the facts about monsters in horse suits right in the beginning. You have to understand the power a horse possesses and don't kid yourself when it comes to the facts. These are facts that can help you avoid trouble in the future if you know what to be on the lookout for.

CHAPTER SIX

TRUST THE PROCESS

It is important to realize that reaching confidence as a rider is a process. A process that will continue to evolve, the more you ride. The process produces the greatest results when you continue to identify and weed out the fears by working at it with a clear goal in mind. As you continue to add new experiences to the mix you will expand your growth. Now that you know the four steps in the process, how far you grow is totally up to you.

It truly is a process. Working with horses is one of the greatest gifts and challenges you will ever take part in. Well, let's just say that has been my experience and what an amazing journey. With each new horse I encountered or took on in my life, I was challenged to face some new fear or unknown situation I had never been in before. Within the process of learning about each new horse and what it would take to find their best for the situation I was in at the time, I would gain a new piece of information or confidence to myself that I didn't have before. Sometimes that new piece of information was an absolute failure on my part, followed by an unexpected lesson I didn't know I needed to learn. But without the failure, I would never have learned the lesson. The lesson contained the confidence to know for sure what to avoid or beware of the next time that kind of horse appeared. The failure also provided the answer that I needed to know, about how to respond when that kind of situation presented itself, that I didn't have before. Some horses and their lessons took longer than others for me to know, but the gift and excitement in meeting each new horse along the way, was like solving a new and exciting mystery. Each one pushed me to expand my riding and horse knowledge skills. The hopes I had about this new horse and the plans I had for the horse within my career goals, all of it, was like purchasing a new ticket to the amusement park each time. At the end of the experience I was left with way more than I bargained for and most times a complete new understanding of how little I truly knew about something. Every single detail of each experience added a new piece of information to my personal world of horse knowledge and skills. Some was good information and some was bad information. The process takes two kinds of information to be able to know with confidence how to handle the situations that will present themselves when you ride and work with horses. Without one, you won't know the other. That's why it is important to learn to trust the process. A mistake or setback is just a lesson you didn't know you needed to learn. A mistake is also what will lead you to find what you are truly after. With each bad experience you are challenged to choose if you realty mean what you were trying to do. Sometimes you need this part of the process to appreciate the type of horse and rider you want to become and the one you want to stay away from. Sometimes you need to know that "hell no" answer and be able to mean it. You can't get to that for sure answer until you have been through the process of both good and bad experiences. You need both of them to know the difference. Just keep loading information into your personal "process" and realize each experience adds a good lesson. Take time to learn the lessons and you will be well on your way to success in your personal confidence growth. Always remember a single day's experience is just that. Tomorrow you can go try again and tomorrow you will be armed with new info.

Each experience you will have with a horse plants one of two things. You either come away with a great experience that adds confidence or a negative experience that creates a doubt. How you handled the situation is an indication of your level of knowledge and applied equestrian skills. That is why you need to trust the process and keep doing the work I explained in each of the four steps. The more you can add to the mix in your experiences and short term small goals, the more opportunity you have to build and grow your confidence in your experience with horses.

Use this book as your guide to refer back to if you get stuck on any one of the steps. This will be your reminder to help you stay on track and remember that riding horses is not about one single day. It is a life long process that you can have a huge affect on with the right information and efforts. Now you have that information, so go to work on it. You will be amazed at what you can accomplish.

How to Gain Confidence as a Rider

A comment from the horse, on the topic of freaking you out in the process:

I am sorry if I freaked you out in fear, but I warned you in the beginning this might happen. I am very straight forward and I aim to please, but next time just take a little more time and get to know me and I will try harder to get to know you. If you are trying to ask me to do things I am scared of myself, then please realize this fact. I need to know you believe we will be ok after the event, before we get into the act. So if you ask me to do something that makes me nervous then please realize I am looking to you for the confidence that we will be ok. If you don't have it yourself, I will sense it in your actions and start looking to make my own exit on my own. And if that requires me pushing and shoving you out of the way to get out of there, then that is what I will do. Each for himself in that case. I don't mean to hurt you, I just need to look out for myself unless I know I can trust you and that takes a lot of time before I sense no doubt in your actions and riding. That's why I like to get you on the ground so I can look you in the eye and we can talk about it first.

And if I kicked you… once again, you probably attempted to impose your will on me without much warning or without much skill and it freaked me out. I have four legs and they are for standing on. If you are attempting to pick one up I need to know about it first, so go slow and let me know what you are up to with some foreplay. I also need to be ready for that physically, so you may need to be in the ready set go position and quick enough to readjust if I get off balance. Once again, I aim to please but seriously, if someone just rolled up on you and grabbed one of your feet off the ground and starting pulling on it what would you do? Exactly.

And if I was a young horse who kicked you as you tried the first few times at teaching me this idea of grabbing my legs was a good idea. Well, that is the dance we are going to have until you explain why that is a good idea for me to participate in. I will need lots of reassurance that you aren't trying to snap my leg off or invade my privacy before I am ready. That is what the dance of trust is going to be about, this single topic. And as long as you aren't listening to the language I'm speaking through my actions you will never gain my trust and it will haunt you every time you try, because I already know I am not going to participate and the fun part will be watching you try. Remember I am bigger than you and there needs to be a good reason for me to do what you are asking, so give me some room to understand by your consistent actions to show me it is a good idea.

How to Gain Confidence as a Rider

So you feel off in front of the jump you had me aimed at? Your fault. I told you that this was about learning to trust and that's what I need to have. I need to know that what you are asking me to do is 100% a good idea, because remember, that was your idea not mine to jump that thing. I obviously wasn't ready or wasn't sure it was a good idea and when I asked you if you were sure, in my subtle hesitation, if we could do it…you gave me no reassurance and actually hesitated in your riding and I sensed it and aborted. If you ask me to take on a mission, make sure you believe in it first or grab one of my school master barn buddies who babysits new riders over the courses, until you get enough confidence to come back and show me why I should jump like they do. We may not be ready for each other just yet. One of us may need some reassurance before we meet again. I will promise you this though. If we conquer the fear together we will be unstoppable as a team and that is what I am looking for. Someone who is willing to hear my side of the story. To that rider I have news for you. I will take you to new heights in your confidence and together we will take on anything. That is what I am looking for, but until then you might keep eating dirt until you learn what I am trying to say. Horses have fears too. Pay attention to our subtle signs when we try to tell you or ask if everything is going to be ok. That is where I am looking for your guidance and if you can be trusted. If you don't answer I will make a move for myself.

Sunny Hale

CHAPTER SEVEN

NEW HABITS THAT WILL HELP YOU

Take some time to think about these next few tips the next time you go ride. If you can start to implement them into your thought process as you ride, they will become your new habits that are much more productive to think about when you ride, than the old messaging that said, "you're doomed."

Using these new tips and focal points over time will also help you start to see things from a horse's perspective and that is part of what I am trying to explain to you in this book, that is so important to start picking up on. Learning about the language a horse speaks can add so much value to your level of confidence, but it takes work to know what to look for. Horses act based on how something is affecting their sense of security. These tips will help you to start kicking your language skills into high gear so you can sense what the horse is thinking, before they ask the question in their physical movements. The earlier you can start to read a situation with a horse, the more time you will have to prepare yourself for what is coming in their moves.

These new habits will help you cut down on the number of unknowns or surprises on your rides. Cutting down the amount of unexpected surprises, will start to build your confidence each time you go riding. Doubts and fear love to live in the space of the unknown, which is why you want to cut them down as much as possible.

Here are a few new tools that can help you do that as you ride. Over time, these small tips and thoughts need to become your new habits, so practice them often until they become your first response in your rides. Think of this chapter as your starter kit to help you build the lasting confidence you are looking for.

> "Pay attention to what type of horse you're riding."

The less training a horse has, the more random their actions will be. The younger the horse, the more rapid and random their actions will be. Horses are naturally built to protect themselves and be aware at all times of impending dangers. The only time they will let their guard down is when they sincerely trust the rider or handler and that is usually only after a long time training together. Well trained horses will trust the scene no matter what their natural born instinct says to do, because the rider they trust has asked them to go there. That is the difference between a really well trained horse and a young or inexperienced horse. The average young horse needs time to learn trust and until they do, they will need reassurance at all times of what you are asking them to do. Which means as the rider, you need to know your stuff or you are asking for trouble. Young horses matched with inexperienced riders spells trouble every time they meet.

"Learn to be aware of your surroundings from the horse's perspective."

The better you can become at reading the surroundings you are in, when you go riding, from the perspective of what the horse is thinking, the better off you will be as a rider. Most people will attempt to say you just need to log hours and put your hands in the right place and your feet in the right place and then you can be called a rider. This is a false sense of security and will uproot your confidence at some point, if you have no idea how to read your surroundings from a different point of view. Thinking of your surroundings as you ride in terms of the horse's thoughts, means you will have a whole new GPS as to what is about to happen in their movements. Once you have a better understanding of how to predict what is to come, you will have some new found confidence that you may have never realized was available to you. You will also have extra time to prepare yourself if something should arise that alarms your horse. Start to use this one thought and you will start to see some clear answers to old mysteries.

How to Gain Confidence as a Rider

"Always pay attention to your gut instinct when you get on an unfamiliar horse."

Your gut instinct is your biggest and best friend, who will always tell you the truth. The minute you swing your leg over a horse's back you will either get an instant feeling of confidence or you will get a line of questions running through your mind. Pay attention to this one detail closely. It is a big clue if this horse is a match for you. When you get a bunch of questions immediately racing through your mind, it may mean that you two are not ready for each other yet.

"Pay attention to a horse's ears, they are your most obvious clue to what the mind is thinking."

Pay particular attention to an ear that stays cocked in one direction. That is where their attention is at the moment and it may have nothing to do with your leg aids. And large warning…if at any point a horse's ears are attempting to touch each other at the tips…you are about to get ejected. Hahaha…I learned that one the hard way ☺!

> *"Make it a new habit to ask more questions about the horse, before you get on it."*

If you are going to ride on an unfamiliar horse, make sure to ask plenty of questions before you get on it. If you are still unsure or have some doubts after asking questions, then ask the person offering it to you, to ride it so you can watch it go for a minute to see how it moves. Use this time to watch the attitude of the horse, the stride of the horse, the gait of the horse, the general frame of mind the horse is in…all of it. Ask lots of questions if you need to and do not be in a hurry to get on until you know the answers. A good horseman will take the time to answer your questions until you are comfortable, so don't be shy. Open your mouth and start asking what you really want to know about the horse and especially if this is a potential horse you are considering purchasing. No question should be out of bounds, so make sure to ask them all.

How to Gain Confidence as a Rider

"Pay attention to the surroundings you are riding in on the horse's behalf. They can have a huge effect on a horse's comfort zone, especially a young horse. "

Young horses like familiar surroundings that they can rely on. When you attempt to take a new or young horse into new surroundings they need a while to gain some confidence, so be prepared for some ducking and diving if this is your situation. This is normal. They are going to ask a ton of questions in their movements until they are sure all is ok. Be prepared to answer their questions and for some of them, you might have to keep repeating the answer. Remember, an inexperienced horse needs time to build confidence too. Always ride with a peripheral vision awareness on the horse's behalf. A lot of times you can save yourself some fun adrenaline rushes of a horse spooking, if you will just keep an eye out and don't leave all the discovering up to the horse. Become a more prepared rider using this one habit.

Sunny Hale

New focal points for you

Here are some additional tips you can start implementing into your new thought process as well, that will help create new fuel in your march to become a more confident rider. You want to start using the ones that apply to you until they become your new habits. Remember this fact. When you are attempting to erase old messaging full of fears and doubts, you have to have new thoughts to fill the old spaces. Once you determine the old "bad messaging" or fears that were creating them, you have to have something "new" to replace the space with or you will fall back into your old habits, that were draining your riding confidence. These new focal points and thoughts are what you will use to start the process and the ones that will start to produce solid confidence that will last. Here are a few that can be very helpful to start focusing on.

- ❖ It is important to have a goal you are working towards. This will fuel your process.

- ❖ Define a single short-term goal or step you are going to go after. One small step at a time. Make this a new focal point.

- ❖ Physically practice at riding, each and every small skill. They will all add up over time.

- ❖ Make a mental note of each step forward, no matter how small the detail may be. Log each one.

- ❖ Focus on small individual steps that seem manageable for where you are in the process.

- ❖ Practice is the key to overcoming stuff that bothers you currently.

- ❖ Reward yourself for progress, no matter how small the step forward is. It is important to realize you are making headway in the battleground. It adds up over time.

- ❖ Focus on new short term goals for yourself.

- ❖ Work on making decisions when you ride so that the horse doesn't have to take over for you. They will fill a blank space if you hesitate too long.

- ❖ The key to productive practice, is to pick a target that you are focused on accomplishing for the ride or the day.

- ❖ With a horse, always remember they have a mind, body and spirit just like you so they have some days that are better than others. Be open to adjusting your plans if necessary.

- ❖ Start small.

CHAPTER EIGHT

ENJOY THE RIDE

Horses will challenge every part of you and your thoughts as you ride them. They have an uncanny ability to read your mood and sense your insecurities without even saying a word to them. Horses have taught me so much and not just about horse training, but about life and myself as well. My experiences with them have taught me more about confidence than any other source. Each thing you are able to learn, yes each individual detail no matter how small, provides you with one more bullet in the gun to kill your fear. This is how you stomp out doubt and fear and it takes time to collect them all.

I have spent the majority of my life working with horses and I have loved every minute of it. I started riding before I can remember walking. Throughout my career I have ridden literally thousands of horses and traveled to 11 countries competing where I competed on horses I had never ridden, much less seen before. The confidence you need to have to be good at polo is about having confidence in the horse you are on. In order to play well, you need to know with confidence that the horse you are riding will run full speed and move itself in inches if necessary in any direction as you challenge other players and horses. You must have confidence to pull the trigger meeting an opponent head on at full speed and confidence that the horse will only do what you ask and no less or more. You also have to know for sure, that you can lean out as far as necessary to take the shot to finish the play. Confidence is a skill that has to be learned. To be the best polo player you can be, you have to be confident in all of your moves on the field at all speeds and be confident in yourself being all over the horse from front to back in the shots and bumps you will take or make with other opponents. It all has to be learned and that takes time.

It is a great journey as you work to become the confident rider you aspire to be, so take your time and enjoy every minute of what you learn along the way. Set out to ride in the places that make you happy and you are confident in. That is the best place to start. When you can take a ride that brings you absolute happiness, it gives you confidence. You need to log a few of those rides to truly start enjoying your overall riding experience. They are the new foundation to your confidence to come. The more of those you can add to your overall experience, the better off your progress will be.

How to Gain Confidence as a Rider

Riding with confidence is the gateway to the adventure of a lifetime. That special connection you will have with a horse is like no other bond. It is powerful. It is encouraging. It is inspirational in each of its moments of growth, no matter how small they may be. It is empowering to both you and the horse. That is the road to confidence and knowledge every horseman has traveled. Enjoy the ride and make your best effort to learn the things you don't know. This is what the experience of a horse will bring, both getting to know them and how to ride them is the adventure of a lifetime, not to be missed. Enjoy your ride and don't forget that the conversation has two participants in your ride from here forward. Do not forget the voice of the horse that has been explained to you. They truly are attempting to communicate with you and the longer it takes you to understand that lesson, the longer it will take to gain the confidence you are looking for. Now that you are armed with a whole lot more information than you had before, you are well on your way to becoming the confident rider you want to be.

Always remember, you are not John Wayne and every horse is not Mr. Ed. Certain types of horses suit certain types of people. You are not meant for every horse type. Monsters in horse suits do exist and you need to be on the lookout for them. Always be wise enough to spot the difference between a horse that needs a trainer for help being reassured and a monster in a horse suit, who would like to remain wild and free.

Knowledge is the key to your confidence. That's why it is so important to trust the process and keep taking the four steps I have lined out for you. Each step holds a piece to your puzzle. Go to work at gaining as much knowledge and experience as you can with each ride. Spend time on the back of a horse as often as possible, even if they are only short rides. With each horse you ride you have a chance to learn something new. With each new thing you learn, you will have one more piece of knowledge. With each new piece of knowledge, you have one more weapon in the war on fear.

Your new homework assignment:

"Go riding…as much as you can."

"Use your new anthem every time a doubt shows up."

"Pay attention to the four steps in the process from here forward."

"Reward yourself for small steps forward…no matter how small they seem in the overall picture."

"Stay focused on your next small goal or step forward you would like to make."

The more riding experiences you can have with this new mindset in place, the faster you will be on your way to becoming a much more confident rider.

I hope this has been helpful for you.

Enjoy your ride and say hello to your horse for me.

Good luck ☺!

Sunny Hale

CHAPTER NINE

ABOUT THE AUTHOR

Sunny Hale

Sunny Hale in action / Photo by Chris Yeo

How to Gain Confidence as a Rider

Sunny Hale

The New York Times called Sunny, "the most famous female polo player in the world."

ESPNW compares her accomplishments as, "Some say she's pulled off the equivalent of being the first woman to earn a World Series ring."

Sunny Hale is widely recognized among her peers in the sport of Polo as the most accomplished and well-respected female polo player in the world. What sets her apart from the pack, is her achievements at the top of what has traditionally been a male dominated sport. Sunny was hired as professional player to compete on teams in the sport of Kings alongside some of the greatest male players in the sport, for over 20 seasons. Her most famous victory in Polo is the day she became the first woman in history to win the US Open Polo Championships as a professional player, hired by the world's Number One Player of all time Adolfo Cambiaso and the Outback Steakhouse Polo Team. The US Open Polo Championships is America's most coveted polo tournament title and trophy. This would be the equivalent of a woman being hired to play in the NBA, World Series or the Super Bowl as a starter among the men and winning the championships. Sunny has competed in 11 countries, is an accomplished horse trainer, teacher and world-renowned equestrian. She is a published author of 3 books and continues to travel the world playing Polo and sharing her message of inspiration to people with a dream.

Sunny has been featured in media and magazines all over the world for her unique and historic accomplishments including ESPNW, Sports Illustrated and the New York Times.

In 2012 she was inducted into the
National Cowgirl Hall of Fame
for her accomplishments.

"The women who shape the West change the world."

The NCHF honors and celebrates women, past and present, whose lives exemplify the courage, resilience, and independence that helped shape the American West. Honorees also include: Sandra Day O'Connor, Georgia O'Keeffe, Annie Oakley and Patsy Cline among others. www.cowgirl.net

To learn more about Sunny go to:
www.sunnyhalepolo.com

Wins and special awards in Polo *(partial list)*

7 Time Polo Magazine Woman Player of the Year

US Open 26 goal: Outback Steakhouse Polo Team
(Adolfo Cambiaso, Sunny Hale, Lolo Castagnola, Phil Heatly *Tim Gannon- team patron)

CV Whitney Cup 26 goal: Lechuza Caracas Polo Team (Pite Merlos, Sebastian Merlos, Victor Vargas, Sunny Hale)

Hall of Fame Cup 22 goal: Outback Steakhouse
 (Adolfo Cambiaso, Gonzalito Pieres, Sunny Hale, Tim Gannon)

Ylvisaker Cup 22 goal & MVP: La Dolfina / Newbridge (Adolfo Cambiaso, Sunny Hale, Matias Magrini, Russ McCall)

Sterling Cup 22 goal: Calumet Polo Team
 (Eduardo Heguy, Nachi Heguy, Henry DK, Sunny Hale)

Robert Skene 20 goal: Goshen Polo Team
 * voted by players **MVP Robert Skene Award**
 (Owen Rinehart, Julio Arellano, Sunny Hale, Ervin Abel)

Bondell Cup 20 goal: Audi Polo Team
 (Gonzalito Pieres, Sunny Hale, Melissa Ganzi, JuanBollini)

Texas Open 20 goal & MVP: Bob Moore Cadillac
International Cup 16 goal: Sympatico Polo Team
Palm Beach Polo & Country Club 14 goal League

Multiple Best Playing Pony Awards

Wins and special awards in Polo *(partial list)*

Women's Polo:

US Women's Open 1990, 2011, 2013 & MVP

WCT Finals 2006, 2007, 2009, 2010, 2011, 2012 & MVP

First Royal Malaysian Ladies Championships 2012

USA vs. Argentina at Palermo Field #1

ICWI International Ladies Tournament Jamaica

Argentine Women's Open 1999

Thai Polo Queen's Cup 2012

Dubai International Ladies Tournament
  *under the patronage of Sheikha Maitha al Maktoum

National Sporting Library Supermatch 2014-15 &MVP

Argentine Women's Open 2015
La Dolfina: SH, Mia Cambiaso, Cande F Araujo, Milagros F Araujo: Coaches: Adolfo Cambiaso & Milo F Araujo

Win of special note:

Don King Days…the famous buckle!
Sheridan Wyoming

Copyright © 2016 Sunny Hale

All rights reserved. No part of this work may be reproduced in any form without the written consent of its author.

www.sunnyhalepolo.com